DIVAS OF POP

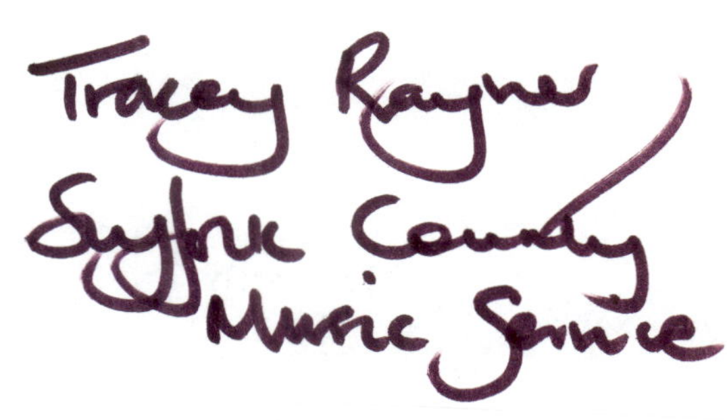

First published by Faber Music Ltd in 2006
3 Queen Square, London WC1N 3AU

Compiled by Lucy Holliday
Designed by Dominic Brookman & Lydia Merrills-Ashcroft
Printed in England by Caligraving Ltd

ISBN 0-571-52558-X

BABY BOY

Words and Music by Sean Henriques, Beyoncé Knowles,
Scott Storch, Robert Waller, Shawn Carter and Ini Kamoze

A♭/C C5

I think a-bout you all the time, I see you in___ my dreams._

A♭/C C5

Ba-by boy, not a day goes by with-out my fan-ta-sies.____

A♭/C A♭ C5

I think a-bout you all the time, I see you in___ my dreams._

Verse 1:

A♭/C C5 A♭/C

1. Ahh, oh, my ba-by's fly ba-by, oh. Yes, no,

C5
Ab/C
C5
hurt me so good, ba-by, oh.
I'm
so
wrapped up in your love, let me go.
Ab/C
Ab
C5
Let me breathe,
stay
out of my fan - ta - sies.
Ab/C
C5
Ab/C
C5
Rap (featuring Sean Paul):
1.2. See additional lyrics
down.
Ab/C
C5
Ab/C
Ab
C5

Chorus:
A♭/C
C5
Ba - by boy, you stay on my mind, ful - fill my fan - ta - sies.
A♭/C
C5
I think a - bout you all the time, I see you in my dreams.
A♭/C
C5
Ba - by boy, not a day goes by with - out my fan - ta - sies.
A♭/C
To Coda ⊕ A♭
C5
I think a - bout you all the time, I see you in my dreams.

Verse 2:
Ab/C
C5
2. Pic-ture us danc-in' real close in a dark, dark cor-ner of a base-ment par - ty.
Ab/C
C5
Ev-'ry time I close my eyes, it's like ev-'ry-one left but you and me. In our
Ab/C
C5
own lit - tle world, the mu - sic is the sun, the dance floor be-comes the sea.
Ab/C
N.C.
Feels like true pa - ra - dise to me.

Chorus:

Ab/C
C5
Baby boy, you stay on my mind, fulfill my fantasies.
Ab/C
C5
I think about you all the time, I see you in my dreams.
Ab/C
C5
Baby boy, not a day goes by without my fantasies.
Ab/C
Ab
C5
I think about you all the time, I see you in my dreams.

Chorus:
A♭/C
C5
Ba - by boy, you stay on my mind.
Ba - by boy, you are so damn fine.
A♭/C
C5
Ba - by boy, won't you be mine.
Ba - by boy, let's con - sid - er lay - ing
A♭/C
C5
down. Ba - by boy, you stay on my mind.
Ba - by boy, you are so damn fine.
A♭/C
A♭
C5
D.S. 𝄋 al Coda
Ba - by boy, won't you be mine.
Ba - by boy, let's con - sid - er lay - ing

Coda

Ab C5 Ab/C

see you in__ my dreams.__

C5 Ab/C C5

Repeat ad lib. and fade

Ab/C C5 Ab/C Ab C5

Rap Intro (Sean Paul):
Certified quality.
A dat da girl dem need and dem not stop cry without apology.
Buck dem da right way, dat my policy.
Sean Paul alongside Beyoncé.
Now hear what da man say.
Dutty Ya, Dutty Ya, Dutty Ya
Beyoncé, sing it now, ya.
(To Verse 1:)

Rap Verse 1 (Sean Paul):
Ya ready gimme da ting dat ya ready get ya live.
And tell me all about da tings that you will fantasize.
I know you dig da way me step da way me make my stride.
Follow your feelings, baby girl, because they cannot be denied.
Come check me in-a night and make we get it amplified.
Me have da ting to run da ship cause I'm go slip and I'm go slide.
And in the words of love I got ta get it certified.
But I give you da toughest longest kinda ride, girl.
(To Chorus:)

Rap Verse 2 (Sean Paul):
Top top, girl
Me and you together is a wrap, dat girl.
Driving around da town in your drop top, girl.
You no stop shock, girl.
Little more da Dutty, we'll rock dat world.
Top top, girl.
Me and you together is a wrap, dat girl.
Driving around da town in your drop top, girl.
You no stop shock, girl.
Little more da Dutty, we'll rock dat world.
(To Chorus:)

BEHIND THESE HAZEL EYES

Words and Music by Kelly Clarkson, Lukasz Gottwald and Martin Sandberg

Original key F♯m

Gm E♭ B♭ F E♭maj7
3fr 6fr 6fr
11
un-break-a-ble, like noth-ing could go wrong. Now I can't breathe no,
Gm7 E♭maj7 F N.C. Gm E♭
3fr 6fr 3fr 6fr
14
I can't sleep I'm bare-ly hang-ing on. Here I am once a-gain I'm
B♭ F Gm E♭ B♭ F
3fr 6fr
18
torn in-to pie-ces, can't de-ny it, can't pre-tend just thought you were the one. Bro-ken up
Gm E♭ Cm7 Gm F E♭
3fr 6fr 3fr 10fr 8fr 6fr
21
deep in-side but you won't get to see the tears I cry be-

B♭
F
Gm
E♭
3fr
6fr
24
hind these ha - zel eyes.
2. I told you ev - 'ry - thing,
op - ened up and let you in,
27
you made me feel all right for once in my life.
Now all that's left of me
30
is what I pre - tend to be:
so to - ge - ther but so bro - ken up in - side.
'Cos
E♭maj7
Gm7
33
I can't breathe
no I can't sleep
I'm bare - ly hang - ing on.

36
F
N.C.
Gm 3fr
E♭ 6fr
B♭
F
Here I am once a - gain I'm torn in - to pie - ces, can't de - ny
39
Gm 3fr
E♭ 6fr
B♭
F
Gm 3fr
E♭ 6fr
it, can't pre - tend just thought you were the one. Bro - ken up deep in - side that
42
Cm7 3fr
Gm 10fr
F 8fr
E♭ 6fr
B♭
F
you won't get to see the tears I cry be - hind these ha - zel eyes.
45
Cm 8fr
B♭ 6fr
Cm 8fr
Gm 3fr
Swal - low me then spit me out. For hat - ing you I blame my - self.

Cm
B♭
Cm(add9)
8fr
6fr
8fr
49
See - ing you, it kills ___ me now, ___ no I don't ___ cry ___ on the out -
E♭maj7
F
Gm
E♭
B♭
F
Gm
E♭
52
- side ___ an - y - more, ___ an - y - more. ___
Fsus4
F
Gm
E♭
B♭
F
56
N.C.
Here I am ___ once a - gain ___ I'm torn in - to pie - ces, can't de - ny ___
Gm
E♭
B♭
F
Gm
E♭
59
___ it, can't pre - tend ___ just thought you were the one. ___ Bro - ken up ___ deep in - side ___ but

Cm7 3fr
Gm 10fr F 8fr E♭ 6fr
B♭ F
62
you won't get to see the tears I cry behind these ha - zel eyes. Here I am
Gm 3fr E♭ 6fr B♭ F Gm 3fr E♭ 6fr
65
once a - gain I'm torn in - to pie - ces, can't de - ny it, can't pre - tend just
B♭ F Gm 3fr E♭ 6fr Cm7 3fr
68
thought you were the one. Bro - ken up deep in - side but you won't get to see the tears I
Gm 10fr F 8fr E♭ 6fr B♭ F
71
cry be - hind these ha - zel eyes.

BIOLOGY

Words and Music by Miranda Cooper, Brian Higgins, Timothy Powell, Lisa Cowling and Giselle Sommerville

2.
A
13
and not my dir - ty brain.
A
1. I got one A - la - ba - ma re - turn
So I got my cap - puc - ci - no to go
G/A
A
17
that - 'll take me far a - way from you, 'cos when you take me in your arms I turn
and I'm head - ing for the hills a - gain, 'cos if we par - ty a - ny - more we'll start
G/A
1.
2.
21
to slave but I can't be saved.
a fi - re of pure de - si - re. Clo -
A
G/A
24
- ser your mind's fir - ing blind with your head in your face get - ting red and your heart beats, clo -
- ser you dive for the thrill at the kill and your heart's had its fill but he still creeps clo -

28
A
G/A
- ser_ you fall_ on your knees_ and the geek_ at your feet_ says you're neat_ and the beat gets clo -
- ser_ you want - ed to freeze but you're weak,_ in too deep and the beat,_ and the beat gets clo -
32
A
- ser,_ clo - ser,_ clo - ser,_ clo - ser,_ clo - ser,_ clo - ser,_ clo - ser._ We
36
A
F♯m
G
D7
give it up and then they take it a - way. A girl's got to
give it up it's just a mat - ter of_ time be - fore_ all the
40
A
F♯m
G
1.
D7
zip it up, and get her head in the_ shade, ba - by, if we
hea - vy stuff comes back to bite your be - hind.

2.
D7
A
F♯m
G
44
You can't mis- take my bi - o - lo - gy (the way that we talk, the way that we walk,
47
it's there in our thoughts). The mag - ic numb- er's in front of me, (the way that we talk,
50
the way that we walk, so eas - i - ly caught). You can't mis- take my bi - o -
53
- lo - gy, (the way that we talk, the way that we walk, it's there in our thoughts).

D7
A
F#m
56
We're gon - na cause a con - tro - ver - sy, (the way that we talk, the way that we walk,
G
D7
A
59
so eas - i - ly caught). Why don't you fool me, feed me,
D/A
A
D/A
A
62
say you need me_ with - out wick - ed games,_ come on and hold me, hug me,
3
3
D/A
1.
A
D/A
2.
A
66
say you love me_ and not my dir - ty brain._ Why don't you and not my dir - ty brain._
3
3

70
F♯m
You can't mis- take my bi - o - lo - gy, (the way that we talk, the way that we walk,
G
D7
A
73
it's there in our thoughts). The mag - ic num-ber's in front of me, (the way that we talk,
F♯m
G
D7
76
the way that we walk, so eas - i - ly caught). You can't mis take my bi - o -
A
F♯m
G
79
- lo - gy, (the way that we talk, the way that we walk, it's there in our thoughts).

D7
A
F#m
82
We're gon - na cause a con - tro - ver - sy, (the way that we talk, the way that we walk,
G
D7
A
D/A
85
so eas - i - ly caught).
3
A
D/A
A
D/A
89
3
3
A
D/A
A
93
3

BRING ME TO LIFE

Words and Music by Ben Moody, Amy Lee and David Hodges

Em
ing some - where cold, un - til you find it there and lead
me. Breathe in - to me and make me real,
Am/E
1.
To Next Strain
N.C.
it back home.
bring
2.
N.C.
To Next Strain
3.
me to life.
me to
Chorus:
Em
G
(3rd time:) life. Wake me up in - side, wake me up in - side.
(Wake me up.) (I can't wake up.)

D Em

Call_ my name_ and save me from the dark._

(Save_ me.)

G

Bid_ my blood_ to run_ be - fore_ I come_ un - done._

(Wake me up.) (I can't wake up.)

D 1. Em *D.S.* 𝄋

Save_ me from_ the noth - ing I've be - come._

(Save_ me.)

2.3. Em C D

noth - ing I've be - come. Bring me to

Em
To Coda
life.
(I've been liv - ing a lie.__)
(There's noth - ing in - side.)
C
D
Em
Bring me to life.
Bridge:
Am
Em/G
B7sus/F♯
Em
Fro - zen in - side__ with-out__ your touch,__ with-out__ your love,______ dar - ling. On-
Am
Em/G
B7sus
D.S. 𝄋 al Coda
ly you______ are___ the__ life____ a - mong__ the dead.______________

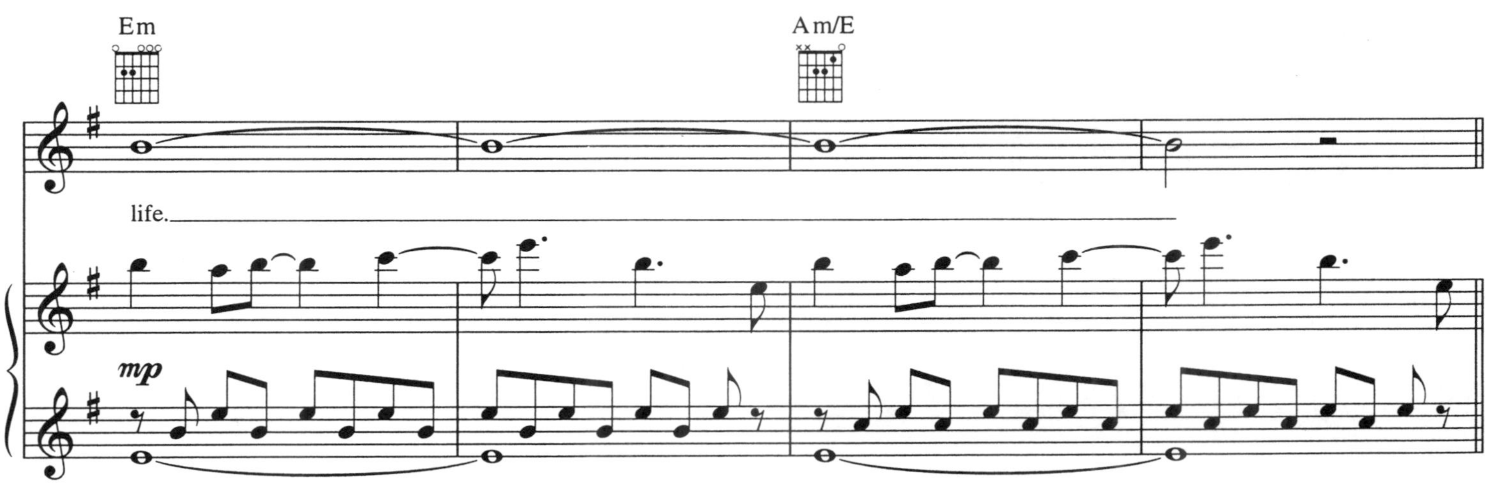

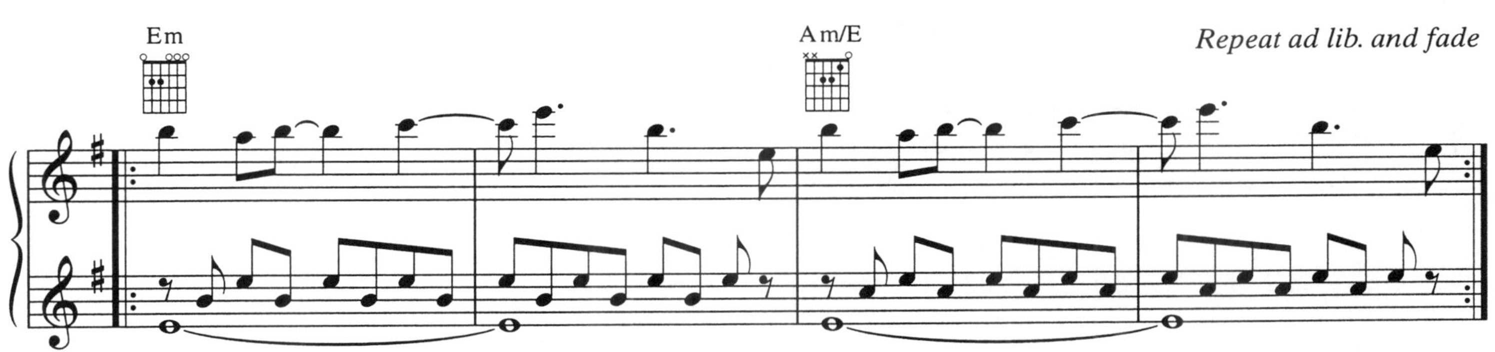

Verse 3:
All this time I can't believe I couldn't see.
Kept in the dark, but you were there in front of me.
I've been sleeping a thousand years, it seems.
Got to open my eyes to everything.
Without a thought, without a voice, without a soul.
Don't let me die here.
There must be something more.
Bring me to life.
(To Chorus:)

CAN'T GET YOU OUT OF MY HEAD

Words and Music by Cathy Dennis and Robert Davis

Dm
F
Am
C
can't get you out of my head; boy, your lov - ing is all I think a-bout. I just
can't get you out of my head; boy, it's more than I dare to think a-bout.
1.
2.
think a - bout.
B♭maj7
A
Ev - - - 'ry night,
There's a dark
G♯dim
Gm
e - - - - ve - ry day,
se - - - - cret in me.
just to be
Don't leave me
4
3

Asus4
A
there in your arms! Won't you
locked in your heart. Set me
Dm7
F
Am9
C
stay? Won't you
free. Feel the
Dm7
F
Am9
To Coda
lay? Stay for
need in me.
B♭maj7
N.C.
D.%.(2º) al Coda
ev - er and ev - er and ev - er and ev - er.

Coda
Dm7
F
set me free.
Am9
Bbmaj7
Stay for ev - er and
ev - er and ev - er and ev - er.
Repeat ad lib. to fade
Dm
F
Am
C
La la la la la la la la. La la la la la la la la.

COME CLEAN

Words and Music by John Shanks and Kara Dio Guardi

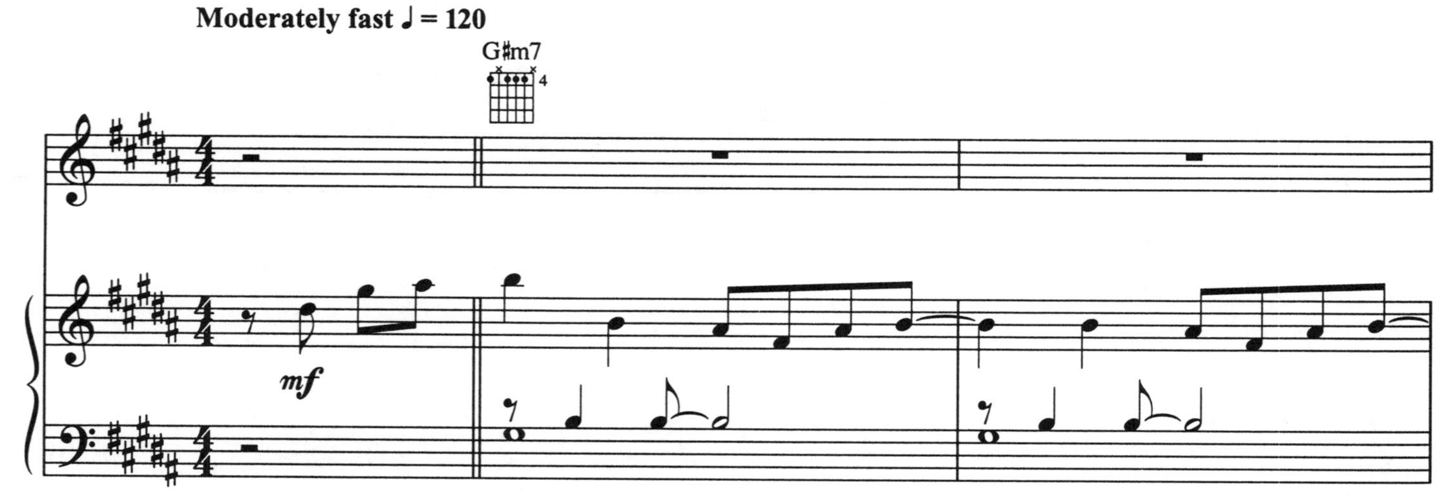

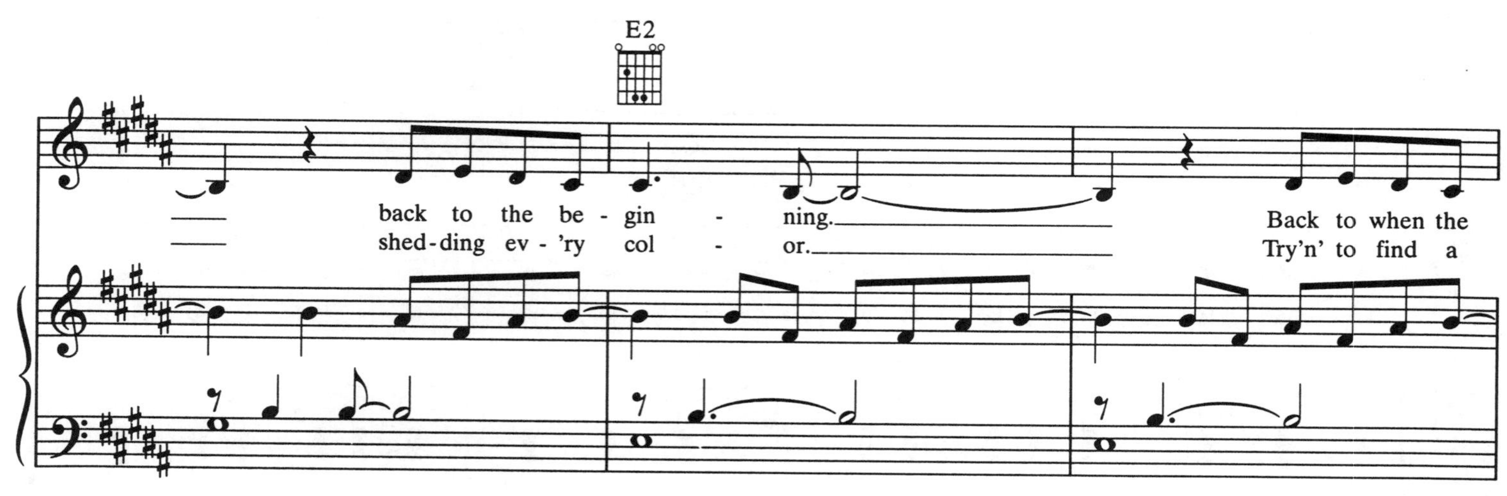

G♯m7
B
E2
earth, the sun, the stars all a-ligned.
pig-ment of truth be-neath my skin.
C♯7sus
G♯m7
'Cause per-fect did-n't feel so
'Cause dif-f'rent does-n't feel so
E2
G♯m7
per-fect. Try'n' to fit a square in-to a cir-
dif-f'rent. And go-in' out is bet-ter than al-
B
E2
C♯9sus
cle was no life. I de-fy.
ways stay-ing in. Feel the wind.

Chorus:
N.C.
G♯m7
Emaj9
Let the rain fall down and
B
F♯
G♯m7
Emaj9
B
C♯
wake my dreams. Let it wash a - way my san - i - ty. 'Cause I wan -
G♯m7
Emaj9
B
F♯
G♯m7
Emaj9 To Coda
na feel the thun - der, I wan - na scream. Let the rain fall down, I'm
B
C♯7
com - ing clean. I'm com - ing

1.
G♯m7
Emaj9
clean.
2.
G♯m7
Bmaj7
2. I'm
clean.
Emaj9
C♯7sus
G♯m7
I'm
com - ing
clean.
(Rain
fall
down,
please.
Rain
fall
Bmaj7
Emaj9
C♯7sus
C♯7
I
hear
rain.
down,
please.
Rain
fall
down.)

G♯m7
Emaj7
B
F♯sus
G♯m7
Emaj7
Let the rain fall.
Let the rain fall.
B
F♯sus
E2
D.S. 𝄋 al Coda
N.C.
I'm com - ing clean.
Let the rain
Coda
B
C♯
Chorus:
G♯m7
Emaj9
B
F♯
(Bkgd voc.)
com - ing clean. Let the rain fall down and wake my dreams. Let it wash
(Lead vocal ad lib.)
G♯m7
Emaj9
B
C♯7
G♯m7
Emaj9
a - way my san - i - ty. 'Cause I wan - na feel the thun - der, I wan -

B F♯ G♯m7 Emaj9 B C♯

na scream. Let the rain fall down. Let the rain

I'm com - ing clean.

C♯9 G♯m7

fall down.

E2 G♯m7

Let's go back,

E2

back to the be - gin - ning.

COMPLICATED

Words and Music by Lauren Christy, David Alspach, Graham Edwards and Avril Lavigne

C(9)
Dsus
D
B♭(9)
Csus
C
And if you could on - ly let it be, you will see
Where you are ain't where it's at. You see, you're mak - ing me
…end solo)
G
Em7
F
Dm7
I like you the way you are when we're driv - ing in your car
laugh out when you strike your pose. Take off all your prep - py clothes.
Chill out, what - cha yell - ing for? Lay back, it's all been done be - fore.
C(9)
Dsus
D
B♭(9)
Csus
C
and you're talk - ing to me one on one. But you be - come
You know you're not fool - ing an - y - one when you be - come
And if you could on - ly let it be, you will see

C(9)
Bb(9)
Em
Dm
some - bod - y else 'round ev - 'ry - one else. You're watch - ing your back like you can't re - lax. You're
C(9)
Bb(9)
D5
C5
try'n' to be cool, you look like a fool to me. Tell me
Chorus:
Em7
Dm7
C(9)
Bb(9)
G
F
Dsus
Csus
D
C
why'd you have to go and make things so com - pli - cat - ed? See, the way you're
Em7
Dm7
C(9)
Bb(9)
G
F
Dsus
Csus
D
C
act - ing like you're some-bod - y else gets me frus - trat - ed. Life's like this, you,

Em7 C(9) G Dsus D
Dm7 B♭(9) F Csus C
you fall and you crawl and you break and you take what you get and you turn it in - to
Am9 C2
Gm9 B♭2
1.
hon - es - ty. Prom-ise me I'm nev - er gon - na find ya fake it. No, no,
G5 C2
F5 B♭2
2.
no. it. No, no,
3. C2 D.S. 𝄋 4. C2
B♭2 B♭2
it. No, no. it. No, no, no.

CAN'T FIGHT THE MOONLIGHT

Words and Music by Diane Warren

A
Em7
un - til, 'til the sun___ goes down.___ Un - der - neath_ the star -
too long 'til you're in___ my arms.___ Un - der - neath_ the star -
D
Em7
D/F♯
light, star - light,___ there's a mag - i - cal feel - ing so___ right.
light, star - light,___ we'll be lost___ in a rhy - thm so___ right.
G
G5
N.C.
Chorus:
Cm
It will take___ you in___ to - night.
Feel it steal___ your heart___ to - night.
You can try___ to re - sist,___ try to hide_
Fm7
B♭
A♭
G
___ from my kiss,___ but you know,___ but you know___ that you can't fight the moon - light. Deep_

Cm
Fm7
in the dark, you'll sur - ren - der your heart. Don't you know,
B♭
A♭
G
Fm7
don't you know that you can't fight the moon - light, no, you can't fight
1.
G7
G/B
2.
G7
it. It's gon - na get to your heart. it.
Fm7
G7
N.C.
No mat - ter what you do the night is gon - na get to you.

Bridge:
Bm7
Em7
A
Can't fight it.
Don't try it, you're nev -
Fm7
er gon - na win, cuz,
un - der - neath the star -
E♭
Fm7
E♭/G
light, star - light,
there's a mag - i - cal feel - ing so right.
A♭
A♭5
It will steal your heart to - night.
You can try

Chorus:
C♯m
F♯m7
B
to re - sist, try to hide from my kiss, but you know, but you know that you
A
G♯
C♯m
F♯m7
can't fight the moon - light. Deep in the dark, you'll sur - ren - der your heart. Don't you know,
B
A
G♯
F♯m7
don't you know that you can't fight the moon - light, no, you can't fight
1.
2.
G♯7
G♯7
it. You can try it. It's gon - na get to your heart.

FALLIN'

Words and Music by Alicia Augello-Cook

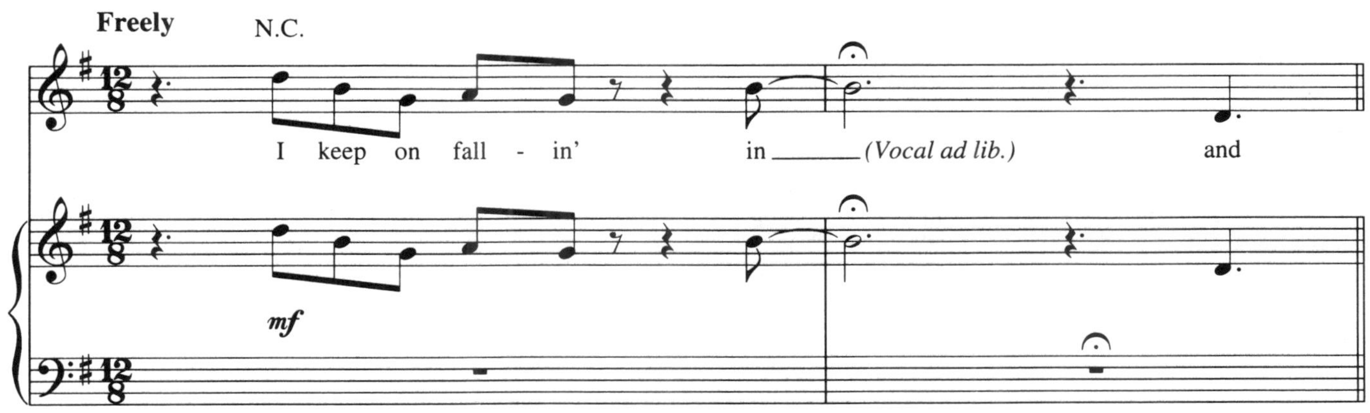

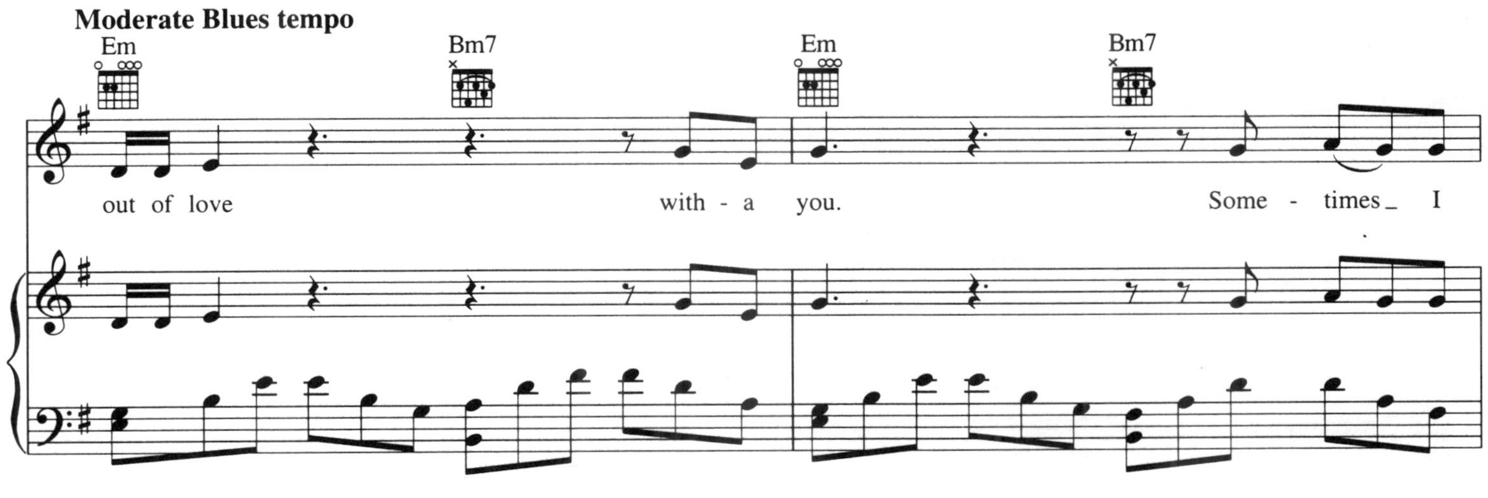

Em
Bm7
Em
Bm7
good. At times I feel used. Lov - ing you
Em
Bm7
Em
Bm7
dar - ling makes me so con - fused. I keep on
Em
Bm7
Em
Bm7
fall - in' in and out of love with - a you. I
Em
Bm7
Em
Bm7
nev - er loved some - one the way that I love a - you. Oh, oh,

Em
Bm7
I never felt this - a
way.
How do you give me so much
pleas - ure and cause me so much pain? Yeah, yeah. Just when I
think I'm tak - ing more than would a fool, I start

Em
Bm7
Em
Bm7
fall - in' back in love with you
I keep on
Em
Bm7
Em
Bm7
fall - in' in and out of love with - a you. I
Em
Bm7
Em
Em/B
B7#9
nev - er loved some - one the way that I love a - you. Oh ba - by.
Em
Bm7
Em
Bm7
I, I, I, I'm fall - in'.

Em Bm7 Em Bm7

I, I, I, I'm fall - in'.

Em Bm7

Fall

Em Bm7 Em Bm7

fall fall.

Em Bm7 Em Bm7

I keep on fall - in' in and out of

Em Bm7 Em Bm7
love with - a you. I nev - er loved some - one the way that
Em Bm7 Em Bm7
I love a - you. I'm fall - in' in and out of
Em Bm7 Em Bm7
love with a - you. I nev - er loved some - one the way that
Em Bm7 Em Bm7
I love a - you. I'm fall - in' in and out of

Em
Bm7
Em
Bm7
love with a - you. I ___ nev - er loved some - one ___ the way that
Em
Em/B
N.C.
Em
Bm7
I love a - you. What?
Em
Bm7
Em
Bm7
Em
Bm7
Em

GENIE IN A BOTTLE

Words and Music by Steve Kipner, David Frank and Pamela Sheyne

D♭
4fr
Fm
E♭
7
N.C.
- tu - ry___ of lone - ly nights, wait - ing for some - one___ to re - lease_
___dance and then we're good to go.___ Wait - ing for some - one___ who needs_
9
N.C.
___ me. You're lick - in' your lips_ and blow - ing kiss - es my way, but that_
___ me. Hor - mones rac - ing at the speed of light, but that_
11
N.C.
___don't mean I'm gon - na give it a - way,_ ba - by, ba - by, ba - by.
___don't mean it's got to be to - night, ba - by, ba - by, ba - by.

D♭
4fr
N.C.
Fm
E♭
Oh,
D♭
Cm7
Fm
E♭
my bo - dy's say - ing, "Let's go!" Oh,
D♭
Cm7
Fm
E♭
Chorus
but my heart is say - ing, "No." If you want to be with
D♭
Cm7
Fm
E♭
me, ba - by, there's a price to pay. I'm a ge - nie in a bot -

21
D♭ 4fr
C7
Fm
E♭
tle, you got - ta rub me the right way. If you want to be with
23
D♭ 4fr
Cm7
Fm
E♭
me, I can make your wish come true.
You got - ta make a big_ im - pres -
Just come and set me
25
D♭ 4fr
C7
To Coda
Fm
E♭
sion, I got - ta like what you do.__
free, and, ba - by, I'll be with you.__ I'm a ge - nie in a bot - tle, ba - by,
27
D♭ 4fr
Cm7
Fm
E♭
you got - ta rub_ me the right_ way, ho - ney. I'm a ge - nie in a bot - tle, ba - by,

1.
2.
D♭
N.C.
come, come, come on and let me out.
2. The
come, come, come on and let me out.
Fm
E♭
D♭
Cm7
I'm a ge - nie in a bot - tle, ba - by, you got - ta rub_ me the right_ way, ho - ney.
I'm a ge - nie in a bot - tle, ba - by, come, come, come on and let me out.
D.𝄋 al Coda
CODA
If you want to be with me, ba - by, there's a price to
4fr

Fm
E♭
D♭
C7
37
pay. I'm a ge - nie in a bot - tle, you got - ta rub me the right
Fm
E♭
D♭
Cm7
39
way. If you want to be with me, I can make your wish come
Fm
E♭
D♭
C7
41
true. Just come and set me free, ba - by, and I'll be with you.
Fm
E♭
D♭
N.C.
43
I'm a ge - nie in a bot - tle, ba - by, come, come, come on and let me out.

GROOVEJET (IF THIS AIN'T LOVE)

Words and Music by Vincent Montana Jr, Ron Walker, Cristiano Spiller, Sophie Ellis-Bextor and Robert Davis

Dm7
(Why does it feel, ah.)
(Why does it feel, ah.)
(Why does it feel, ah.)
Am
Why does it feel so good?
Dm7
If this ain't love.
(Why does it feel, ah.)
G
(Why does it feel, ah.)
(Why does it feel, ah.)
Why does it feel so good?

Am
G9sus4
C
Em7
Will you re - mem-ber me, boy?
Re - mem-ber me, boy, will you
Am7
Am
re - mem - ber?
Am
3. Just for this life - time you can be my pas - time, here are the rules of our

Dm7
play.
In it to-geth - er 'til I know you bet - ter.
Darling, dar - ling, now what do you say.
Am
If this ain't love.
Dm7
(Why does it feel, ah.) (Why does it feel, ah.) (Why does it feel, ah.)
Am
Dm7
(Ah.) (Why does it feel, ah.) (Why does it feel, ah.)

Am
(Why does it feel, ah.) Why does it feel so good?
If this ain't love.
Dm7
(Why does it feel, ah.) (Why does it feel, ah.) (Why does it feel, ah.)
G
Am
Why does it feel so good?
If this ain't love.

G9sus4
C
Em7
Why does it feel so good?
Am7
Am
Dm7
Am
Am
Repeat to fade
Perc.

HERE WITH ME

Lyrics by Dido Armstrong
Music by Dido Armstrong, Paul Statham and Pascal Gabriel

Bm
it might change my me-mo-ry.
risk for-get-ting all that's been.
Em
Oh, I am what I am, I'll do what I want. But
F♯m
I can't hide. And I won't go,
G
I won't sleep, I can't breathe
D
un-til you're rest-ing here with me.
Dmaj7
And I

Bm
3
won't leave, and I can't hide, I can - not
1.
A
be un - til you're rest - ing here with me.
2,3.
A
be un - til you're rest - ing here. And I won't
G
D
go, and I won't sleep, and I can't breathe un - til you're

Dmaj7
Bm
rest - ing here with me. And I won't leave, and I can't
Asus4
A
To Coda
hide, I can-not be un - til you're rest-ing here with me.
Em7
F♯m
D.𝄋. al Coda
Oh, I
Coda
Em7
F♯m

HUNG UP

Words and Music by Madonna, Stuart Price, Benny Andersson and Björn Ulvaeus

Dm
F
Am
Ev-'ry lit-tle thing that you say or do, I'm hung up, I'm hung
up on you.
Wait-in' for your call, ba-by, night and day, I'm fed up,
To Coda
N.C.
I'm tired of wait-in' on you.
1. Time goes by so
slow-ly for those who wait, no time to hes-i-tate.
Those who run seem to

31
have all the fun, I'm caught up, I don't know what to do.
34
Time goes by so slow-ly. Time goes by so slow-ly.
38
D.%. al Coda
Time goes by so slow-ly, I don't know what to do.
Coda
Dm
F
Am
42
Ev-'ry lit-tle thing that you say or do, I'm hung up, I'm hung

45
Dm
F
up on you.
Wait-in' for your call ba-by night and day, I'm fed up,
48
Am
Dm
N.C.
I'm tired of wait-in' on you.
2. Ring, ring, ring goes the
51
te-le-phone, the lights are on but there's no-one home.
Tick, tick, tock, it's a
55
quar-ter to two, and I'm done,
I'm hang-ing up on you.

B♭
F
A
Dm
58
I can't keep on wait - ing for you,
62
I know that you're still he - si - ta - ting.
66
Don't cry for me, 'cos I'm find - - ing my way,
70
you'll wake up one day but it-'ll be too late.
3
3

Dm
F
Am
74
Ev-'ry lit-tle thing_ that you say or do, I'm hung up, I'm hung-
77
up on you._
Wait-in' for your call_ ba-by night and day, I'm fed up,
80
I'm tired of wait-in' on you._
83
86
repeat to fade

I'M LIKE A BIRD

Words and Music by Nelly Furtado

B♭
F
E♭maj9
5
I won't ev - er trade.
you don't know me that well.
And tho' my love is rare,
F6
E♭
3
F
yeah, and tho' my love is true,
B♭
F6
I'm like a bird, I'll on - ly fly a - way.
I don't know where my
Cm
3
E♭
3
soul is, I don't know where my home is.
(And ba - by all I need for you to

B♭
F6
I'm like a bird, I'll on-ly fly a - way. I don't know where my
know is:)
Cm
1.
E♭
soul is, I don't know where my home is. 2. Your
(All I need for you to know is:)
2.
E♭
E♭maj9
home is. (And ba - by all I need for you to know is:)
It's not that I wan-na say good - bye,
Gm7
6
E♭maj7
F
it's just that ev-'ry time you try to tell me, me, that you love me, oh, oh,

E♭maj9
Gm11
E♭maj9add6
each and ev - 'ry sin - gle day, I know I'm gon - na have to e - ven - tu - al - ly give you a -
F
E♭maj9
- way, yeah, yeah, yeah, yeah. And tho' my love is rare, rare, rare,
F6
F
E♭
F
and tho' my love is true, yeah, I'm just
E♭
F6
F
E♭
scared, yeah, yeah, and tho' we may fall through-woo-woo-woo-woo-woo-woo-woo - woo,

F6
F
B♭
yeah, yeah, yeah, yeah.
I'm like a bird,
F6
Cm
I don't know where my soul is,
I don't know where my
E♭
B♭
home is.
(And ba - by all I need for you to know is:)
I'm like a bird,
I'll on - ly fly a -
F6
Cm
- way
I don't know where my soul is,
I don't know where my

E♭
B♭
home is. (And ba - by all I need for you to know is:)
I'm like a bird, I'll on - ly fly a -
F6
Cm
- way I don't know where my soul is, I don't know where my
E♭
B♭
home is. (And ba - by all I need for you to know is:)
I'm like a bird, I'll on - ly fly a -
F6
Cm
E♭
Repeat to fade
- way I don't know where my soul is, I don't know where my home is. (And ba-by all I need for you to

INNOCENT EYES

Words and Music by Vince Pizzinga and Delta Goodrem

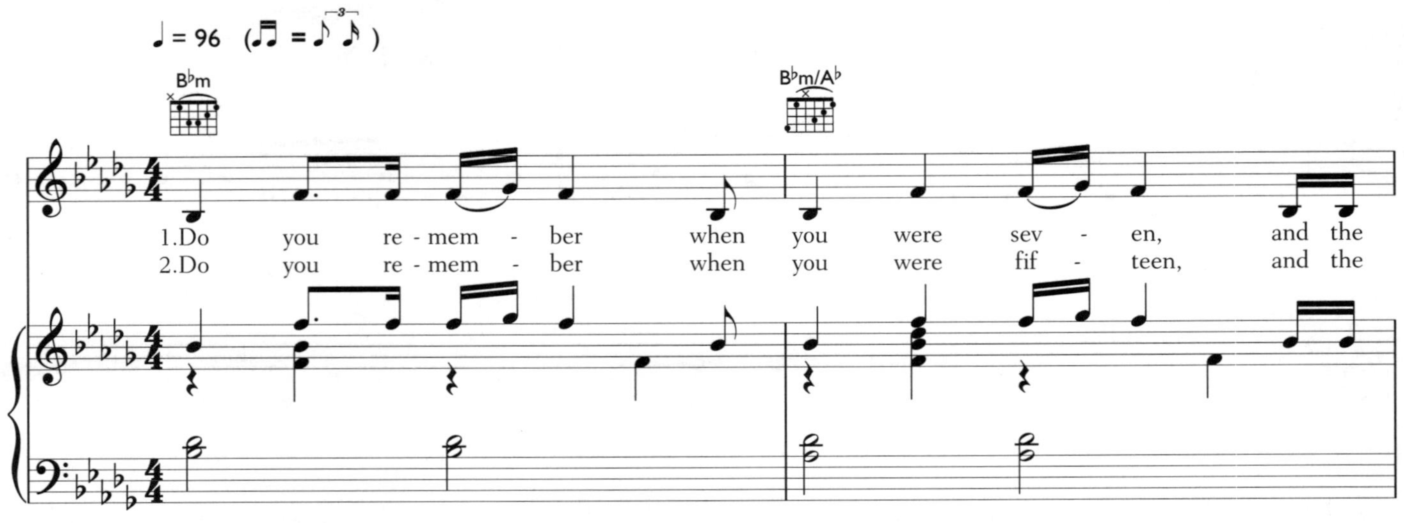

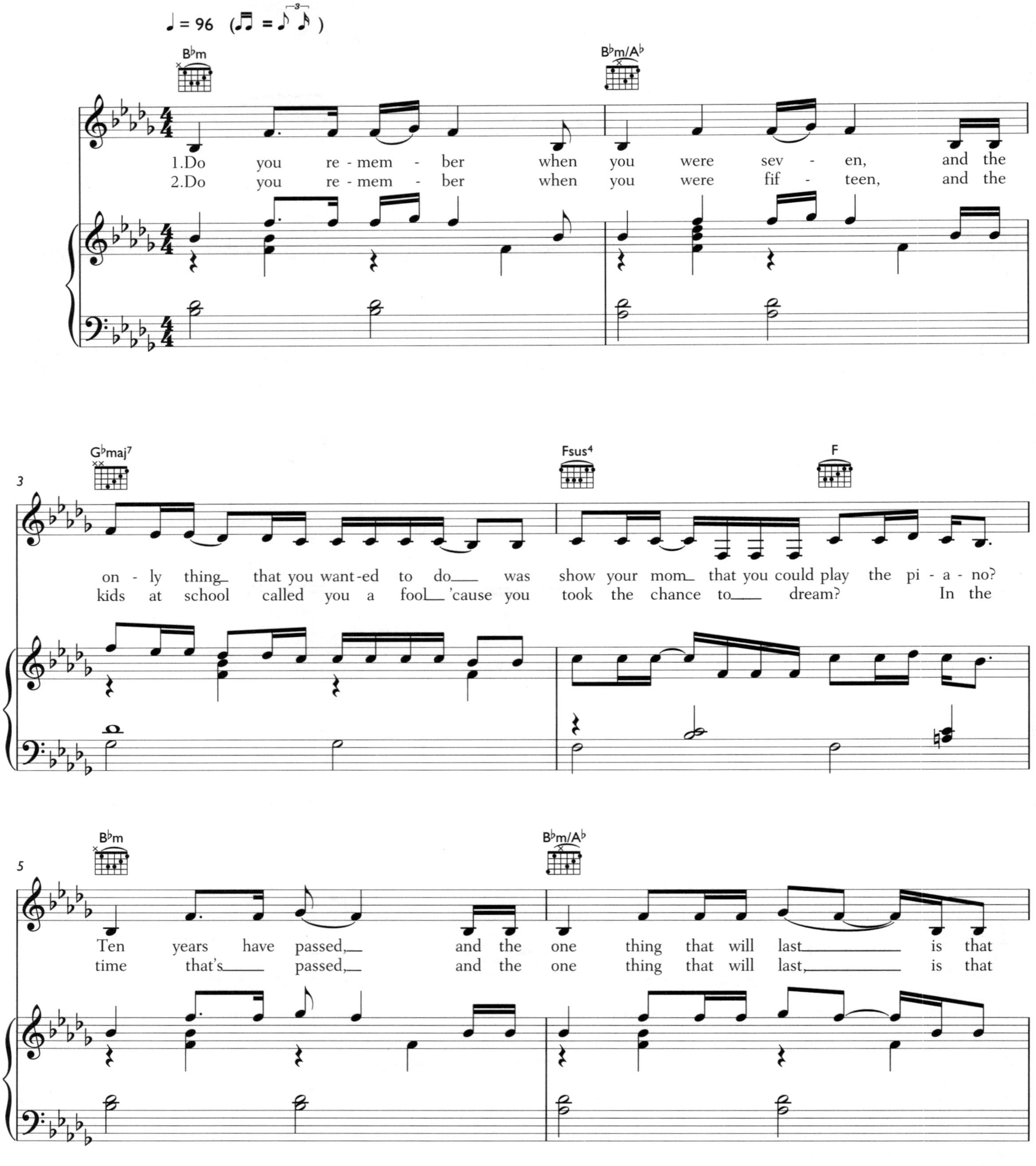
♩ = 96
B♭m
B♭m/A♭
1.Do you re - mem - ber when you were sev - en, and the
2.Do you re - mem - ber when you were fif - teen, and the
G♭maj7
Fsus4
F
3
on - ly thing that you want-ed to do was show your mom that you could play the pi - a - no?
kids at school called you a fool 'cause you took the chance to dream? In the
B♭m
B♭m/A♭
5
Ten years have passed, and the one thing that will last is that
time that's passed, and the one thing that will last, is that

G♭maj7
Fsus4
F
same old song that we played a - long that made my mom - ma cry.
same old song that we played a - long that made my dad - dy cry.
Am
F
E
I miss those days, I miss those ways, when
Am
F
E
I got lost in fan - ta - sies, in a car - toon land of mys - te - ries, in a
place you won't grow old, in a place you won't feel cold. And I'll sing
3

Am
F
G
Em
15
(Da - da - da - da da - da da - da - da - da da - da). Seems I'm lost in my re -
17
- flec - tion. (Da - da - da - da da - da da - da - da - da da - da). Find a star for my di -
19
- rec - tion. (Da - da - da - da da - da da - da - da - da da - da). For the lit - tle girl in -
21
- side, who won't just hide. Don't let me see mis - takes and lies, let me keep my

1.
2.
G
Em
To Coda
E
F
A/C♯
24
faith in in - no - cent eyes.
Un - der my feel - ings, un -
Dm
F
A/C♯
Dm
27
- der my skin
un - der the thoughts,
or with - in.
F
A/C♯
Dm
F
A/C♯
Dm
30
Learn-ing the sub - text of the mind
See cre - a - tion, how we're de - fined
Am
D. 𝄋 al Coda
34
Ped.
Ped.

Coda
Am F G Em
36
(Da - da - da - da da - da da - da - da - da da - da). Faith in in - no - cent eyes.
Am F G Em Am F
38
(Da - da - da - da da - da da - da - da - da da - da). Faith in in - no - cent eyes. (Da - da - da - da da - da da - da - da - da
G Em Am F G Em
41
da - da). For the lit - tle girl in - side, who won't just hide Don't let me see mis - takes and
Am F G Em Am
44
lies, let me keep my faith in in - no - cent eyes.

OVER THE RAINBOW

Words by E Y Harburg
Music by Harold Arlen

D♭
D♭m7
A♭
A♭/G
in a land
and the dreams
Fm
B♭m7
E♭7sus4
E♭7/G
that I heard of once, once in a lul -
that you dared to dream real - ly do
A♭add9
1.
B♭m7
E♭/G
2, 3.
B♭m7
E♭/G
- la - by.
come true.
Some
A♭add9
A♭5
A♭add9
A♭5
A♭add9
A♭5
A♭add9
A♭5
B♭m7
B♭7sus4
B♭m7
B♭7sus4
day I'll wish up-on a star and wake up where the

E♭7/G E♭/G E♭7/G E♭/G A♭maj9 Fm
clouds are far be - hind me.
B♭m7 B♭m9 Cm/E♭ B♭m/E♭ A♭add9 A♭5 A♭add9 A♭5
Where trou - bles
A♭add9 A♭5 A♭add9 A♭5 G7
melt like le - mon drops a - way a - bove the chim - ney tops, that's
Cm Cm/B B♭m7 E♭7/G
To Coda
D.%. al Coda
where you'll find me.

Coda
rit.
B♭m7
E♭7/G
me.
a tempo
A♭5
Fm
Cm7
A♭7
Some - - - - where ov - er the rain - bow
D♭
D♭m7
A♭add9
A♭7
A♭sus4/B♭
A♭/C
skies are blue, and
D♭
D♭m7
A♭
A♭5/G
Fm
the dreams that you dared to

rit.
a tempo
B♭m7
E♭7sus4
E♭7/G
A♭add9
A♭5
dream real - ly do come true. If
hap - py lit - tle blue - birds fly a - bove the rain - bow,
B♭m7
B♭7sus4
rubato
a tempo
E♭/G
D♭add9
why, oh why can't I?
A
rit.
A♭

JUST LIKE A PILL

Words and Music by Alecia Moore and Dallas Austin

E5
D5
5fr
E5
3
sup - port, there's a short-age in the switch. I can't stay on your mor - phine, 'cause it's mak-ing me itch.
D5
5fr
E5
I said I tried to call the nurse a - gain, but she's being a lit - tle bitch.
D5
5fr
E5
To Coda
A5
5fr
I think I'll get out of here, where I can run just as fast as I can
F♯5
D5
5fr
E5
to the mid-dle of no - where, to the mid-dle of my frus - trat - ed fears. And I

A5
F#5
D5
5fr
swear, you're just like a pill. 'Stead of mak-ing me bet-ter, you keep mak-ing me ill,
E5
A5
F#5
you keep mak-ing me ill. Run just as fast as I can to the mid-dle of no-where,
D5
E5
A5
to the mid-dle of my frus-trat-ed fears. And I swear, you're just like a pill.
F#5
D5
E5
D.S. al Coda
'Stead of mak-ing me bet-ter, you keep mak-ing me ill, you keep mak-ing me ill.

CODA
A5
F#5
run just as fast as I can to the mid-dle of no-where,
D5
E5
to the mid-dle of my frus-trat-ed fears. And I
A5
F#m
D5
swear, you're just like a pill. 'Stead of mak-ing me bet-ter, you keep mak-ing me ill,
Repeat and Fade
E5
you keep mak-ing me
Optional Ending
E5
A5
you keep mak-ing me ill.
5fr

NO MORE DRAMA

Words and Music by Terry Lewis, James Harris, Barry De Vorzon and Perry Botkin Jr

F♯(add2)
F♯m
E(add2)
E
D(add2)
D
2fr
ooh,
no more, no more.
Umm,
Spoken: I'm so tired.
Tired, tired of all this drama.
hey
ooh,
well.
Bro - ken heart a - gain,
an - oth - er les - son learned.
Bet - ter know your friends
or else you will get burned.
Got - ta count on me

D(add2)
D
F♯(add2)
F♯m
F♯(add2)
F♯m
'cause I can guar - an - tee that - a I'll be fine. No more
F♯(add2)
F♯m
F♯(add2)
F♯m
E(add2)
E
pain. No more pain. No more pain. No more
E(add2)
E
D(add2)
D
pain. No dra - ma,
(No more dra - ma in my life.
D(add9)
D
F♯(add2)
F♯m
no more in my life.
No - one's gon - na make me hurt a - gain,

F♯(add2)
F♯m
ooh.)
Why'd I play the fool,
E(add2)
E
go through ups and downs, knowing all the time you would-n't be a-round?
D(add2)
D
2fr
But may-be I like the stress, 'cause I was young and rest-less.
But that was long a-go.
N.C.
I don't wan-na cry no more.
No more
pain.
tears.
No more
No more

E(add2)
E
E(add2)
E
D(add2)
D
game.
fears.
No drama,
D(add2)
D
F♯(add2)
F♯m
1
F♯(add2)
F♯m
no more in my life.
No more
2
F♯(add2)
F♯m
E/G♯
Gon-na speak my mind, o-kay.
Ooh, it feels so good when you
Dmaj7
E/G♯
G♯m7
C♯7
let go of all the dra - ma in your life. Now you're free

Dmaj7
F#m
from all the pain.
Free from all the game
Free
Dmaj7
Amaj7
G#m7
4fr
C#7
from all the stress,
so bide your hap - pi - ness.
F#(add2)
F#m
F#(add2)
F#m
E(add2)
E
I don't know,
on - ly God knows where the stor - y ends
for me.
But - a
E(add2)
E
D(add2)
2fr
D
I know where the stor - y be - gins.
It's up to us to choose.

D(add2) 2fr D F♯(add2) F♯m

Whether we win or lose. And I choose to win,

F♯(add2) N.C. 3 3 3 3 F♯(add2) F♯m

ooh. No more {1. 3. pain. / 2. tears.

3 3

F♯(add2) F♯m E(add2) E E(add2) E

No more game.}
No more fears.} No dra-

D(add2) 2fr D D(add2) 2fr D F♯(add2) F♯m

ma, no more in my life.

1, 2
F♯(add2) F♯m

3
F♯m(add2) F♯m E/G♯

No more No __ more. __ No more

A C♯7 F♯m E/G♯ A C♯7 C♯7♯9

dra - ma. No more dra - ma.

F♯m E/G♯ A C♯7 C♯7♯9 F♯m E/G♯ Dmaj7

No more dra - ma. No more dra - ma.

F♯m E/G♯ A C♯7 F♯m E/G♯ A C♯7 C♯7♯9

No more dra - ma. No more dra - ma.

F♯m
E/G♯
A
C♯7
C♯7♯9
F♯m
E/G♯
No more dra - ma.
No more
Dmaj7
F♯m
E/G♯
A
C♯7
dra - ma.
No more dra - ma.
F♯m
E/G♯
A
C♯7
F♯m
E/G♯
No more dra - ma.
Oh no. Oh no,
Dmaj7
C♯m7
Bm7
A(add9)
G♯m7
C♯7sus
4fr
no more, no more, no more dra - ma.
No more dra - ma in my, in my

F♯m(add2) F♯m F♯m(add2) F♯m E(add2) E
life. I'm so tired,
Spoken: I'm so tired.
E(add2) E D(add2) D D(add2) D F♯m(add2) F♯m
2fr
so tired. Go a-head, let go the dra-ma, well, well.
So tired of all this drama
Repeat and Fade
F♯m(add2) F♯m F♯m(add2) F♯m F♯m(add2) F♯m E(add2) E
E(add2) E D(add9) D D(add9) D F♯m(add2) F♯m F♯m(add2) F♯m
Optional Ending

PUSH THE BUTTON

Words and Music by Dallas Austin, Keisha Buchanan, Mutya Buena and Heidi Range

E
A
wan-na feel his bo-dy I can't re - sist it. I know my hid-den looks can
be de - cei - ving but how ob-vi-ous should a girl be? I was
Bm
E
ta-ken by the ear-ly con-ver - sa-tion piece, and I real-ly like the way that he
A
re-spect-ed me. I've been wait-ing pa-tient-ly for him to come and get it, I

27
Bm
wonder if he knows that he can say it and I'm with it? I knew I had my mind made up from
30
E
the very be-gin-ning catch this op-por-tu-ni-ty so you and me could feel it. 'Cos
33
A
if you're rea-dy for me boy you bet-ter push the but-ton let
36
Bm
me know be-fore I get the wrong i-dea and go you're gon-na

E
39
A
miss the freak that I con - trol.
2. I'm bu - sy show-ing him what
42
he's been miss - ing, I'm kind of show-ing off for his full at - ten - tion, my
Bm
45
E
sex-y ass has got him in the new di - men-sion, I'm rea-dy to do some-thing to re-lieve this mis - sion.
A
49
Af-ter wait-ing pa-tient-ly for him to come and get it, he came on through and asked me if I want-ed to get with him, I

Bm
E
53
knew I had my mind made up from the ve-ry be-gin-ning, won't miss this op-por-tu-ni-ty so you and me could feel it. 'Cos
A
57
if you're rea-dy for me boy you bet-ter push the but-ton let me know be-fore I
Bm
E
61
get the wrong i-dea and go you're gon-na miss the freak that I con-trol.
A
65
Bm
E
69

A
Af-ter wait-ing pa-tient-ly for him to come and get it, he came on through and asked me if I wan-ted to get with him, I
Bm
E
knew I had my mind made up from the ve-ry be-gin-ning won't miss this op-por-tu-ni-ty so you and me could feel it. 'Cos
A
if you're rea-dy for me boy you bet-ter push the but-ton let me know be-fore I
Bm
E
repeat and fade
get the wrong i-dea and go you're gon-na miss the freak that I con-trol.

REDNECK WOMAN

Words and Music by John Rich and Gretchen Wilson

C7
G
D7
I can't swig that sweet cham-pagne. I'd rath-er drink beer all night in a tav -
ern, or in a hon-ky-tonk, or on a four-wheel-drive tail - gate.
I've got post - ers on my wall of Sky-nyrd, Kid and Strait. Some
peo-ple look down on me, but I don't give a rip. I

C7
N.C.
stand bare - foot - ed in my own front yard with a ba - by on my hip. 'Cause I'm a
Chorus:
G
red - neck wom - an, I ain't no high - class broad. I'm just a
prod - uct of my rais - in'. I say, "Hey, y'all," and "Yee haw!" And I
C7
keep my Christ - mas lights on on my front porch all year long. And

G
I know all the words to ev - 'ry
Char - lie Dan - iels
Tan - ya Tuck - er
Ol' Bo - ce - phus
song. So
D7
here's to all my sis - ters out there, keep - in' it coun - try.
C
N.C.
To Coda
C
Let me get a big "Hell yeah!" from the red - neck girls like
B♭
G
1.
me. Hell yeah! (Hell yeah!)

2.
2. Vic - to - ri - a's)
C7
(Inst. solo ad lib....
G
C7
A7
D7
D.S. 𝄋 al Coda
...end solo) I'm a

Verse 2:
Victoria's Secret,
Well, their stuff's real nice.
Oh, but I can buy the same damn thing
On a Wal-Mart shelf, half price
And still look sexy,
Just as sexy as those models on TV.
No, I don't need no designer tag
To make my man want me.
You might think I'm trashy,
A little too hard-core,
But in my neck of the woods,
I'm just the girl next door.
(To Chorus:)

RIGHT TO BE WRONG

Words and Music by Desmond Child, Betty Wright and Joss Stone

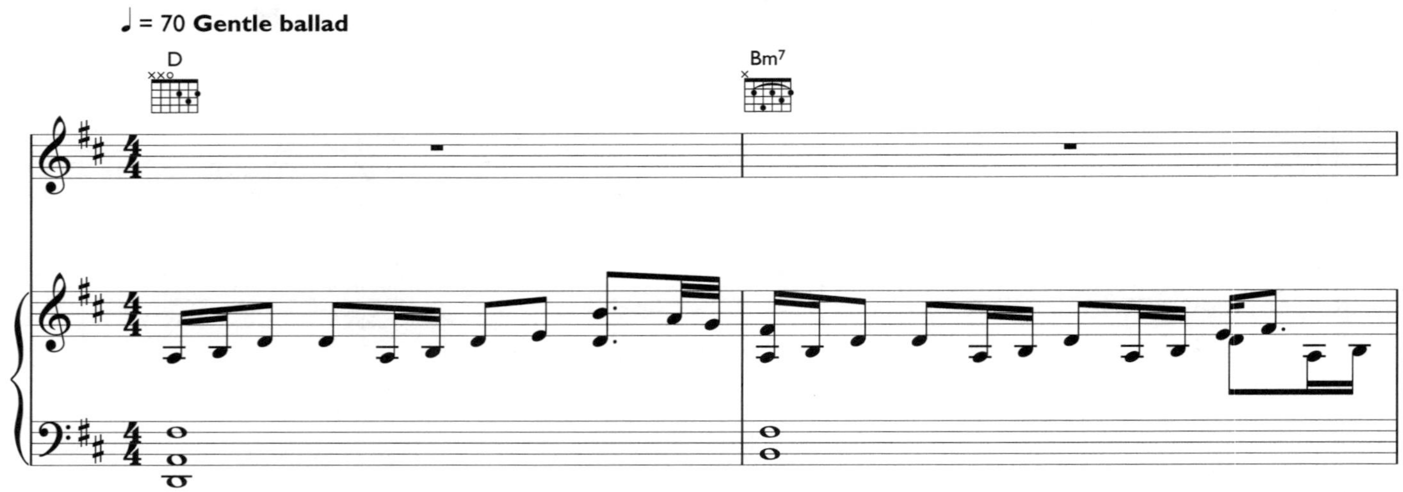

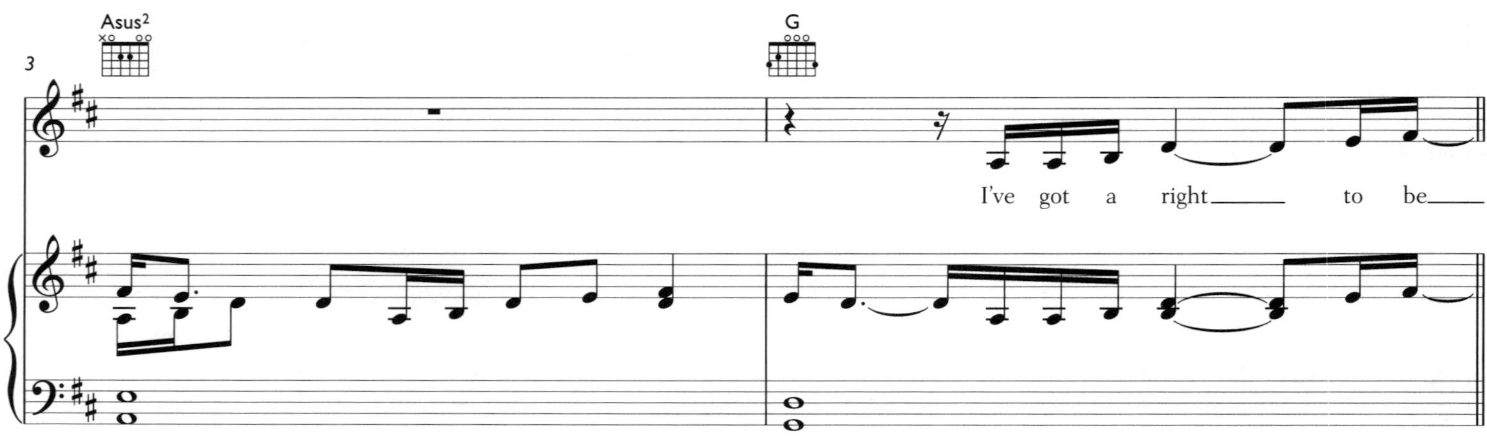

D
Bm7
7
make me strong.
I'm step-ping out into the
A
G
9
great un - known,
I'm feel-ing wings though I've ne-
5
D
Bm7
11
- ver flown.
Got a mind of my
A
G
13
own,
I'm flesh and blood

15
D
Bm7
to the bone, I'm not made of stone.
Got a right to be
17
A
G
N.C.
wrong,
so just leave me a - lone.
19
A5
D
21
A
Got - ta right to be wrong,
I've been held down too long,

G
D
Bm7
A
G
D
Bm7
A
5
I've got to break free so I can fi - nal - ly breathe.
Got a right to be wrong, got - ta sing my own song,
I might be sing - in' out - ta key but it sure feels good to
me. Got a right to be wrong,

1.
G
N.C.
D5
2fr
so just leave me a - lone.
A
G7
You're en - ti - tled to your o - pin - ion, but it's real - ly my de - ci - sion. I
D7
Bm7
can't turn back I'm on a mis - sion, if you care, don't you dare blur my vi - sion.
Am
A
G
Let me be all that I can be, don't smo - ther me with ne - ga - ti - vi - ty.

D7
A7
A7sus4
What-ev-er's out there wait-ing for me, I'm gon-na face it will-ing-ly!
Oh!
2.
G
N.C.
Got a right to be so just leave me a-lone.
D
Bm7
Asus2
G
D

SICK AND TIRED

Words and Music by Dallas Austin, Glen Ballard and Anastacia Newkirk

Dm
Csus2
G
A lit-tle late for all the things you did-n't say,
No warn-ing of such a sad song
I'm not sad for you.
of brok-en hearts.
But I'm sad for all the time I had to waste
My dreams of fai-ry tales and fan-ta-sies
'cause I learned the truth.
were torn a-part.
Your heart is in a place I no long-er wan-na be,
I lost my peace of mind some-where a-long the way,

Dm Csus2 G Dm
I knew there'd come a day I'd set you free 'cause
I knew there'd come a time you'd hear me say
I'm sick and tired of
Csus2 G Dm Csus2 G
al-ways be-ing sick and tir - ed.
(De la li a bib bot a wah de la de. De la li a bib bot a wah de la de.)
Am C G Dm Am C
Your love is-n't fair, you live in a world where you did-n't lis-
G Dm Am C G Dm
-ten and you did-n't care. So I'm float - ing, I'm float-ing on air.

1.
F
G6
To Coda
Dm
(La li a bib bot a wah de la_ de. De
Csus2
G
Dm
Csus2
G
I'm_ on_ air._
la li a bib bot a wah de la_ de. De la li a bib bot a wah de la_ de. De la li a bib bot a wah de la_ de.)
2.
F
G
F
My love_ is_ on the line, my love_ is_ on the line. My love_ is_ on the line,
G
Am
C
G
Dm
my love_ is_ on the line.

Am C G Dm Am C
(La li a bib bot a wah de la de. De la li a bib bot a wah de la de.)
My love is on the line,
D.%.al Coda
Coda
G Dm Am C G Dm
my love
Your love is-n't fair, you live in a world
Am C G Dm Am C
where you did-n't lis - ten and you did-n't care. So I'm float-
G Dm Am C G Dm
N.C.
-ing, I'm float-ing on air
I'm float-ing, I'm float-ing on air.

SUNRISE

Words and Music by Lee Alexander and Norah Jones

Cm Ab Eb Cm Bb Eb Ab
11
af - ter - noon's al - rea - dy come and gone. And I said "Ooo,
Cm Bb Eb Ab
14
ooo,
Cm Bb Eb Ab Fm7 Bb Cm
17
ooo," to you. Sur - prise, sur - prise, could - n't
Bb Eb Cm Eb Ab Eb
21
find it in your eyes, but I'm sure it's writ - ten all o - ver my face. Sur -

Gm Cm B♭ E♭ Cm A♭
24
-prise, sur-prise, ne-ver some-thing I could hide, when I see we made it through an-oth-er day,
E♭ Cm B♭ E♭ A♭ Cm B♭ E♭ A♭
27
then I say "Ooo, ooo,
Cm B♭ E♭ A♭ Fm7
31
ooo", to you.
B♭ Cm B♭ E♭ Cm E♭ A♭
35

E♭ Gm 3fr Cm 3fr B♭ E♭
Cm 3fr A♭ 4fr E♭ F/A
Now the night,
A♭ 4fr F/A A♭ 4fr
will throw its cov-er down, mmm on me a-gain,
F/A A♭ 4fr F/A
oo and if I'm right, it's the on-ly way to

A♭
Cm
B♭
E♭
A♭
Cm
B♭
E♭
A♭
50
bring me back.
"Ooo,
ooo,
Cm
B♭
E♭
A♭
Fm7
54
ooo"
to you.
Cm
B♭
E♭
A♭
Cm
B♭
E♭
A♭
58
"Ooo,
ooo,
Cm
B♭
E♭
A♭
Fm7
E♭
62
ooo",
to you

SITTING DOWN HERE

Words and Music by Lene Marlin Pedersen

G
3fr
A
words cut rath-er deep - ly, they're just some oth - er lies I'm
(2.) try-ing to a - void you, just don't wan-na hear your voice, when you
with pedal
D
A
G
3fr
hid-ing from a dis - tance, I have got to pay the price. De - fend-ing all a - gainst it, I
call me up so of - ten I don't real-ly have a choice. You're talk-ing like you know me and
A
Bm7
real - ly don't know why, you're ob - sessed with all my se - crets, you
wan - na be my friend, but that's real - ly too late now, I won't
A
G
3fr
A
al-ways make me cry. You (1,3.) seem to wan-na hurt me, no mat-ter what I do, I'm
try it once a-gain. You may think that I'm a los - er, that I don't real - ly care, may
(with pedal)

D
A/C#
Bm
A
tell - ing just a cou - ple, but some - how it gets to you. But I've
think that it's for - got - ten, but you should be a - ware. 'Cause I've
G
3fr
A
Bm
G
3fr
learned to get re-venge and I swear you'll ex - pe - ri - ence that some day. I'm
learned to get re-venge and I swear you'll ex - pe - ri - ence that some day.
D
5fr
A
5fr
Em
7fr
sit - ting down here but hey, you can't see me, kind - a in - vi - si - ble, you don't
no pedal
G
3fr
A
5fr
D
5fr
A
5fr
sense my stay. Not real - ly hid - ing, not like a sha - dow, just

1.
Em 7fr
Bm7 7fr
A 5fr
D 5fr
thought I would join you for one day. I'm sit - ting down here but hey,
A 5fr
G 3fr
you can't see me, (see me, see me, see me, see me.) 2. I'm not
2.,3.
D 5fr
A 5fr
Em 7fr
sit - ting down here but hey, you can't see me, kind - a in - vi - si - ble, you don't
G 3fr
A 5fr
D 5fr
A 5fr
sense my stay. Not real - ly hid - ing, not like a sha - dow, but

Em
7fr
Bm7
to Coda ⊕
A
5fr
D
A
sure I wan-na join you for one day.
(Acoustic guitar)
Em
G
3fr
A
D
A
Em
D.𝄋 al Coda
G
A
3. You
⊕ CODA
Bm7
A
D
day.
I'm sit-ting down here but hey,
A
Em
G
A
you can't see me,
kind-a in-vi-si-ble, you don't sense my stay.

D
A
Em
5fr
7fr
Not real - ly hid - ing, not like a sha - dow, just thought I would join you for one
Bm7
A
D
A
day. I'm sit - ting down here but hey, you can't see me,
Em
G
A
D
3fr
kind - a in - vi - si - ble, you don't sense my stay. Not real - ly hid - ing, not
repeat to fade
A
Em
Bm7
A
like a sha - dow, but sure I wan - na join you for one day. I'm

STRICT MACHINE

Words and Music by Alison Goldfrapp, William Gregory and Nick Batt

B♭5
D♭5
when told what to do.
what I want so please.
1, 2. Won - der - ful e - lec - tric,
3° Instrumental
F5
A♭5
won - der - ful e - lec - tric,
To Coda
won - der - ful e - lec - tric,
co - ver

A♭5
G♭5
F5
N.C.
me,
you.
I'm in love,
A♭5 B♭5
I'm in love,
I'm in love with a strict ma - chine.
I'm in love,
I'm in love,
I'm in love
with a strict ma - chine.
1.
N.C.
When you send

2.
N.C.
D.%.al Coda
I'm in love.
Coda
N.C.
A♭5
B♭5
I'm in love, I'm in love, I'm in love
with a strict ma - chine. I'm in love, I'm in love,
I'm in love with a strict ma - chine. I'm in love,
Repeat to fade

SUPERSTAR

Words and Music by Mich Hansen, Joseph Belmaati and Mikkel Sigvardt

E♭m
got a feel - ing I'll see you lat - er.
Bad boys on their best be - ha - viour.
There's some - thing
There's some - thing
E♭m
'bout this,
'bout you
let's keep it mov - ing,
and if it's good let's just get some - thing
cook - ing,
'cause I real - ly wan - na rock with you.
D♭
I'm
feel - ing some con - nec - tion to the things you do.
E♭m
N.C.
(You do, you do.)
I don't know

E♭m
25
what it is that makes me feel like this, I don't know who you are, but you must
28
D♭
be some kind of sup - er - star, 'cause you got all eyes on you no mat - ter
31
E♭m
To Coda
where you are. (You just make me wan - na play.)
E♭m
I like the way you're mov - ing,
34
(ey oh, ey oh, ey oh.) I just get in - to the grove and then (you just make me wan - na play.)

37
D♭
E♭m
If you just put pen to pap - er, (ey oh, ey oh, ey oh.) Got that feel-ing I'll see you lat - er.
40
N.C. (E♭)
Make your move, can we get a lit - tle clos - er?
(ey oh, ey oh, ey oh.)
43
(D♭)
You rock it just like you're sup-posed to. Hey,
D.𝄋 al Coda
(ad lib. vocal)
46
(E♭)
boy I ain't got no-thing more to say 'cause you just make me wan - na

Coda
49
E♭m
I don't know what it is that makes me
(you just make me wan - na play.).
51
feel like this, I don't know who you are, but you must be some kind of
54
D♭
E♭m
sup - er - star, 'cause you got all eyes on you no mat - ter where you are.
1.
2.
57
I don't know (You just make me wan - na play.)
(you just make me wan - na)

SWEET DREAMS MY L.A. EX

Words and Music by Cathy Dennis, Pontus Winnberg, Christian Karlsson and Henrik Jonback

B♭
A
11
— no - one cares but you.
— all you dreamed and more?
C
B7
B♭7
13
What pla - net are you from?
Ac - cuse me of things that I
A
C
16
— ne - ver done.
List - en to you carry - ing on,
B7
B♭7
A
19
cheat - ing an - oth - er love song.

Dm
B♭
If I were in your shoes, I'd whis - per be-fore I
shout.
Dm
Can't you stop play - ing that re - cord a - gain? Find
B♭
A
some - bo - dy else to talk a - bout.
Dm
B♭
If I were in your shoes, I'd wor - ry of the ef -

A
Dm
32
- fects. You've had your say but now it's my turn,
B♭
A
35
sweet dreams my L. A. ex.
Am7
D7
Gm7
3fr
C7
37
Does it make you feel a man, point - ing the fin - ger be - cause you can?
Am7
D7
Gm7
3fr
C7
B7
B♭7
41
I'll spell it loud and clear: Ba - by that tongue's not wel - come a - round here.

A
Dm
B♭
45
You turned the ci - ty 'round. (L. A. ex.) D'you think I give a damn?
A
48
(L. A. ex.) D'you think that I'm the fair - er
Dm
B♭
N.C.
50
S - E - X? Sweet dreams my L. A. ex.
A
Dm
B♭
53

A
Dm
56
B♭
A
59
Dm
B♭
61
If I were in your shoes, I'd whis - per be-fore I
A
Dm
64
shout. Can't you stop play - ing that re - cord a - gain? Find

67
B♭
A
some - bo - dy else to talk a - bout
69
Dm
B♭
If I were in your shoes, I'd wor - ry of the ef -
72
A
- fects You've had your say but now it's
74
Dm
N.C.
my turn. sweet dreams my L. A. ex.

THESE WORDS

Words and Music by Stephen Kipner, Andrew Frampton, Natasha Bedingfield and Wayne Wilkins

F
Dm
Dm C/E F
8
I try to foc - us my at - ten - tion, but I feel so A - D - D.
B♭
F
10
I need some help, some in - spi - ra - tion, but it's not com - ing ea - si - ly.
Not 2°
Gm
Dm
Gm
3fr
12
Try'n to find the mag - ic, try'n to write a clas - sic, don't you know? Don't you know?
Dm
Gm
Dm
15
Don't you know? Waste bin full of pap - er, clev - er rhymes see you lat - er.

F
Dm
C/E
F
B♭maj7
18
These words are my own, from my heart flow, I
F
C
F
21
love you, I love you, I love you, I love you. There's no o - ther
Dm
C/E
F
B♭maj7
F
C
23
way to bet - ter say I love you, love you.
F
Dm
C/E
F
B♭maj7
26
These words are my own, from my heart flow, I

29
F
C
F
love you, I love you, I love you, I love you. There's no o - ther
31
Dm
C/E
F
B♭maj7
F
C
To Coda
way to bet - ter say I love you, love you.
34
N.C.(Dm)
I'm get-ting off my stage, the cur-tains pull a-way. No
36
hy - per-bole to hide be-hind My nak-ed soul ex - pos - ed.

39
Woah, woah, woah, woah, woah.
Gm
3fr
42
Dm
Try'n to find the mag - ic, try'n to write a clas - sic,
Gm
3fr
44
N.C.
D.𝄋 al Coda
(no repeats)
waste bin full of pap - er, clev - er rhymes see you lat - er.
Coda
F
46
Dm
C/E
F
These words are my own, they're from my heart

Verse 2:
Read some Byron, Shelley and Keats
Recited it over a hip-hop beat.
I'm having trouble saying what I mean
With dead poets and drum machines
You know I had some studio time booked
But I couldn't find a killer hook
Now you're gonna raise the bar right up
Nothing I write is ever good enough.

TOXIC

Words and Music by Cathy Dennis, Pontus Winnberg, Christian Karlsson and Henrik Jonback

Cm
1.
2.3.
8va
Pre-chorus:
1. Too high, can't come down.
2. Too high, can't come down.
Los - in' my head, spin - nin'
It's in the air and it's
E♭
G
'round and 'round.
all a - round.
Do you feel me now?
Can you feel it now?
Cm
N.C.
8va

Chorus:
Cm
Eb7
Oh, the taste of your lips, I'm on a ride.
D7
Db7
Cm
You're tox - ic. I'm slip - pin' un - der.
Oh, the taste of a poi - son
Eb7
Ab
G7(#9)
Db7
par - a - dise. I'm ad - dict - ed to you. Don't you know that you're tox - ic?
Cm
Eb7
D7
And I love what you do. Don't you

D♭7
Cm
E♭7
know that you're tox - ic?
1.
A♭
G7(♯9)
D♭7
D.S. 𝄋
2.
A♭
G7(♯9)
N.C.
Don't you know that you're tox - ic?

Oh, the
Chorus:
Cm
E♭7
D7
taste of your lips, I'm on a ride. You're tox - ic.
D♭7
Cm
E♭7
I'm slip - pin' un - der.
Oh, the taste of a poi - son par - a - dise. I'm ad -

1.
2.
A♭
G7(♯9)
D♭7
Cm
E♭7
D7
N.C.
dict - ed to you. Don't you know that you're tox - ic?
know that you're tox - ic?
In - tox - i - cate me now, with your lov - in' now.
I think I'm read - y now.
I think I'm ready now.
In - tox - i - cate me now,
with your lov - in' now.
I think I'm read - y now.
8va

WHOLE AGAIN

Words and Music by Andrew McCluskey, Stewart Kershaw, Bill Padley and Jeremy Godfrey

B
E
B
Bsus4
B
cry, but you can make me whole a - gain.
E
C♯m
2. If you see me with an-oth-er man, laugh-ing and jok - ing, do - ing what I can,
3. Time is lay-ing hea-vy on my heart, seems I've got too much of it since we've been a - part.
C♯m/B
A
B
I won't put you down, 'cos I want you a - round, and you can make me
My friends make me smile, if on-ly for a while; you can make me
E
B
Bsus4
B
E
whole a - gain.
whole a - gain.
Look-ing back on when we first met, I can-not es-

B
A
-cape and I can-not for-get.
Ba-by you're the one, you still turn me
B
E
1.
B
Bsus4
B
2.
B
Bsus4
B
on, and you can make me whole a-gain.
A
C♯m
B
C♯m
Spoken: So now I'll have to wait, but baby if you change your mind don't be too late, 'cos I just can't go on,
A
B
E
Bsus4
B
Badd9
B
it's already been too long, but you can make me whole again.

E
B
3
Look-ing back on when we first met, I can-not es-cape and I can-not for-get.
A
B
Ba-by you're the one you still turn me on, and you can make me
E
1.
B
Bsus4
B
2.
B
whole a-gain. Huh, woh. Oh ba-by you're the
A
N.C.
E
one, you still turn me on, you can make me whole a-gain.

THEY

Words and Music by Ward Swingle, Jem Griffiths and Gerard B. Young Jr

Fm
C7(no3)
13
1. Who made up all the rules? We fol - low
2. And it's i - ro - nic too, coz what we
16
them like fools. Be - lieve them to be true,
tend to do is act on what they say,
19
don't care to think them through.
and then it is that way.
Fm/B♭
B♭m
E♭
E♭/A♭
A♭
C7(no3)/F
21
I'm sor - ry, so sor - ry, I'm sor - ry it's like this.

25
Fm
Fm/B♭
B♭m
E♭
E♭/A♭
A♭
Fm
Fm/B♭
B♭m
I'm sor - ry, so sor - ry, I'm sor - ry
28
C7(no3)
C7(no3)/F
Fm
1.
Fm
C7(no3)
we do this.
30
Fm
C7(no3)
Fm
C7(no3)
Fm
C7(no3)
2.
33
Fm
C7(no3)
Fm
C7(no3)
Fm
C7(no3)
Fm
C7(no3)
Who are_ they? Where are_ they? How can_ they pos - si - bly know all this?

37
C
Fm/C
Dm7(no5)/C
C
C
Fm/C
Dm7(no5)/C
C
41
Fm
Fm/C
C
C7(no3)
Gm(no5)/F
Fm
Fm/Bb
Bbm6
Do you see what I see? Why do we
44
C
C/F
Fm
Fm
Fm/C
C
C7(no3)
Gm(no5)/F
Fm
live like this? Is it be - cause it's true
47
Fm/Bb
Bbm6
C
C/F
Fm
Fm/Bb
Bbm
that ig - no - rance is bliss? Who are they?

E♭
E♭/A♭
A♭
Fm
Fm/B♭
B♭dim
C7
C7/F
Fm
50
Where are they?
How do they
know all this?
Fm/B♭
B♭m
E♭
E♭/A♭
A♭
Fm
Fm/B♭
B♭dim
C7
C7/F
Fm
53
I'm sor - ry,
so sor - ry.
I'm sor - ry
it's like this.
we do this.
Fm
Fm/C
C
C7(no3)
C7/F
Fm
Fm/B♭
B♭m6
C7(no3)
C7(no3)/F
Fm
57
Fm
Fm/C
C
C7(no3)
C7(no3)/F
Fm
Fm/B♭
B♭m6
Bdim7
Fm/C
C
61